THE ART OF SHITO-RYU KARATE

José Luis Calderoni

with technical supervision from

Master Kunio Murayama

WRITTEN BY JOSE CALDERONI ELIAS
WITH THE COLABORATION OF MARCELO CALDERONI
SUPERVISED BY MASTER KUNIO MURAYAMA.
WITH THE APPROVAL OF MASTER MANZO IWATA.

Photography by: Antonio Rodríguez González
and Adolfo Calderoni

CONTENTS

Born in Miyagi prefecture, Japan in 1944, Shihan Murayama began his formal training in Shitoryu in 1962 after enrolling into Toyo University. A direct student and 'uchi-dashi' (live in disciple) of the great master and former president of Shito-kai, Shihan Manzo Iwata, Murayama sensei was exposed to a great deal of knowledge and information and excelled in his study of karatedo.

Even after graduating with a degree in economics, Murayama stayed at the university to coach and captain his university team, gaining a number of national awards in various tournaments. Wishing to become a professional karate instructor, and on being offered a chance to pioneer karate outside Japan, in 1970 Murayama Sensei moved with his wife and young family to Monterrey in the Mexican state of Nuevo Leon. There, over the decades that followed, Murayama Sensei would coach the Mexican national team that competed in the 3rd world karate championships in Long Beach, California; establish his own dojo, teach countless students to black belt; mentor many champions, and become a respected World Karate Federation Referee and Kata judge.

His contribution to karate's development in Central America and beyond is without doubt. Master Kunio Murayama 8th Dan, WSKF, now in his 5th decade of karate, continues to work tirelessly to ensure the information learned from his teacher, Manzo Iwata, continues to be passed on to future generations as accurately and faithfully as possible. A quiet and unassuming man, generous and modest by nature, patient and understanding, Murayama Sensei has proved to be a stalwart of traditional Shito-ryu karate-do, epitomising what a master of karatedo should be, as embodied in the phrase, 'Kunshi no Ken', a 'gentleman of karate'.

KARATE

Karate is the philosophical method of combat and technique to protect the physical and spiritual integrity of a person, whose body coordination transform him into the purest of weapons, he removes any unnecessary movements from his technique and becomes as efficient and effective as possible. The art of Karate can be beneficial for physical training, spiritual development or as self defense. It is necessary to train every technique in a conscious manner to be able to understand the essence of Karate as a martial art.

The real value of Karate comes from the effectiveness of its training in the physical abilities of the human body and from its meaning as a spiritual discipline. This is the true meaning of Karate and all other martial arts.

More important than technique or power, its the spiritual element which allows you to move and react with freedom in any circumstance.

To rule, a man must first rule himself. Without knowing yourself Karate will lead to frustration, by knowing yourself you will learn to understand and value other people.

The purest of feelings will be manifested by this medium. This feelings are bravery, courage, justice, unbreakable will, respect and the desire for personal growth.

KARATE-DO

空 = *KARA: Empty, philosophical principle of Zen.*

手 = *TE: Hand, technique.*

道 = *DO: Road, way.*

HISTORY OF KARATE

In China approximately 3,000 years B.C. there was a form of physical training wich was closely related to Kempo, the chinese method of hand to hand combat. In itself we can estimate that Kempo was systematized around 2,000 years B.C.

In the third century, a famous surgeon of the time created a combat system by combining the old chinese physical training method and Chinese Kempo. For this new combat system he got his inspiration from five different animals: the tiger, the bear, the deer, the monkey and the birds.

In the year 520 A.D. a monk named Bodhidharma (Daruma Taishi in Japan) the founder of Zen Buddhism traveled from India to China and settled in the Shaolin-ssu (Shorin-ji in Japanese) monastery in the Hunan province near tsou-jyo where he taught Zen buddhism.

It is said that after seeing that his students couldn't handle the intense physical demands of his teachings, often passing out from exhaustion, he put his students under a special physical and mental regimen to better condition them to withstand his training.

At first there were only three "forms" or Kata* and this then were split into five each Kata supposedly mimicking a different animal; the dragon, the tiger, the leopard, the snake and the crane. However Chinese culture demands a story to explain for certain traditions that is why it is not known for sure if this forms were really based on these 5 animals or if it is a myth to fulfill these demands.

The five animal names may have been used as a way of describing and relating certain principles of the forms such as speed, body movement, agility, fluidity and calmness. This art spread throughout China in just a few years.

The techniques brought by Bodhidharma to China became known as Shaolin-ssu Kempo (Shorinji Kempo in Japanese) and they spread from China to other asian countries after war developed between them, some of this countries were Mongolia, Korea, Vietnam, Taiwan and more.

The art of Karate was developed in a small island named Ryu-Kyu located in Okinawa. Ryu-Kyu already had its own unarmed combat system called TE*. When Okinawa started dealing commercially with China, Chinese Kempo and the art of TE* started mixing. But it was until the year 1,500 A.D. when Karate started to develop as a complete martial art.

Karate, the empty hand fighting method, was the method used by those who were forbidden by the authorities to own or use any kind weapons. Throughout oriental history there have been instances where people have risen against the authorities and fought against them with their bare hands.

In the year 1470, Shopasi, who controlled the islands of Okinawa filed a decreet that stated that the ownership or possession of any kind of weapon was illegal and if caught punishable by death.

Later, in 1609, lord Shimazu who belonged to the Satsuma province (Clan Satsuma) invaded Okinawa and continued the prohibition of arms. With this occupation by the Satsuma Clan who were evicted from Japan after being defeated in the 1600's civil war, the art of TE was developed even further. In contrast with the round movements that were incorporated into the art by its Chinese influence, the art of TE mostly consisted of straight and hard techniques and incorporated a solid training method for the practitioners to be able to hit vital points they had to be able to go through their enemy's wooden armor with their bare hands and feet.

This is how the weapons deprived inhabitants of Okinawa perfectioned the art of fighting bare handed, Karate. Trained in the two most important cities of Okinawa, Shuri and Naha, Karate opened way for two schools Shuri-te* and Naha-te*.

Shuri-te had Anko Itosu for its teacher and he taught the Kata Nai-huan-chi (Naifanchi), the system of Shuri-te is characterized by its straight and fast movements. Naha-te had Kanryo Higaonna as the teacher and he taught the Kata Sanchin, the system of Naha-te is characterized by its round movements and difference of speeds. These two masters are now regarded as the two most influential characters of Okinawan Karate.

THE DOJO

The word Dojo can be translated as "place for the way" meaning a place where you practice your philosophical method. A Dojo is more than just a gym; a gym only denotes the physical aspect of training while the Dojo involves not only the physical but the spiritual as well.

The Karate Dojo only consists of a floor of polished and treated wood to be able to move freely while barefoot. The Karate uniform or Karate-gi consists of a light white coat and pants and a belt that indicates your advancement in the art by wearing different colors. The Karate-gi must be completely white indicating pureness and the only thing that should be allowed to be added is the Dojo's symbol or flag.

Behavior inside the Dojo should be very strict and formal in its interaction with other practitioners. The instructors should always be refered at as Sempai and the teacher or maximum authority in the Dojo should always be refered at as Sensei.

You should always bow before entering or leaving the Dojo, and to the instructor when meeting him or saying goodbye. This creates a good relationship between student and teacher.

Before and after training, students line up in front of the instructor whose heels are together and toes apart (Musubi-Dachi) and back is against the front of the Dojo, then the instructor turns his back to the students to face the front of the Dojo. The order Seiza is given which means to kneel in a certain way for your bottom to rest on your heels and your hands relaxed over your legs. After Seitza, the order Mokuso is given, which refers to a meditation where you close your eyes for approximately 1 minute, then at the order of Mokuso Yame you stop the meditation and open your eyes, Then the order Rei is given and you bow down by placing your hands on the floor. After this the instructor will turn to face the students and another order will be given to bow down again in the same manner by saying (name of the teacher) Sensei ni Rei, if there is another instructor in attendance another order will be given by saying (name of the instructor) Sensei (or Sempai) Rei. Finally the order Kiritsu is given and you stand up to the position of Musubi-Dachi only after the instructor and your superiors (more advanced students) have done it first. The most advanced student in attendance will be the one giving the orders.

BEFORE AND AFTER TRAINING MEDITATION

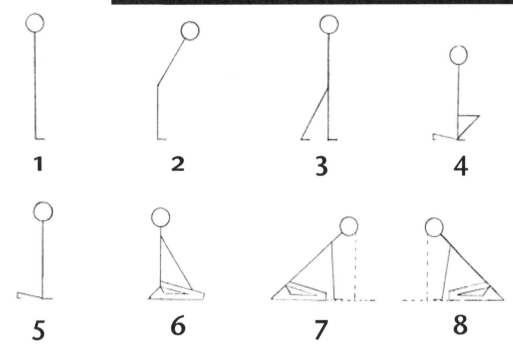

1 2 3 4

5 6 7 8

STEPS:

1) Musubi-Dachi
2) Bow
3) The left foot is placed behind you
4) The left knee is placed on the floor
5) The right knee is placed on the floor
6) Seiza position
7) Bow down for respect, once for the Dojo, and once for the teacher

6) Seiza position
5) Kneeling position
4) Right foot is placed on the floor
3) Stand up
2) Move the right foot to meet the left one and form Musubi-Dachi position, bow
1) Musubi-Dachi

WEAPONS OF THE BODY

SEIKEN (fist)

Roll your fingers toward the palm of your hand and squeeze tight, place your thumb on top of the first two fingers. This way the whole hand solidifies minimizing the risk of injury and becomes more harmful when you strike your opponent. Only use the first two knuckles of your hand.

NAKADAKA IPPON KEN

After forming the seiken stick out the middle finger second knuckle. With this method you can focus all your power in a small area such as the temple, the eyes, the throat, the solar plexus or the ribs.

HITOSASHI IPPON KEN

The same concentration of power can be acquired with the index finger second knucle.

HIRA KEN

By folding only the second knuckles of the fingers and leaving the hand in an extended position you can strike areas like the solar plexus or the nose bridge.

URA KEN *(back of the fist)*

Use this by striking with the back of the first two knucles of your fist.

KEN-TSUI *(bottom of the fist)*

Commonly referred as hammer fist. Both the top or bottom of the fist can be used.

YON HON NUKITE *(open hand with four fingers)*

Commonly referred as spear hand, with the hand completely extended and fingers close together slightly bend the middle finger so that the index, middle and ring finger form a straight line. With the hand in this position you strike with your fingertips.

NI HON NUKITE *(hand with two extended fingers)*

Index and middle fingers extended to strike with the fingertips.

IPPON NUKITE *(hand with one extended finger)*

Index finger extended while the other fingers are bent on the second knuckle.

SHUTO *(knife hand)*

Hand and fingers completely extended and the thumb bent inwards. Strike by using the side of your hand opposite from your thumb.

SHOTEI

With the hand completely extended bend the second knuckles of your fingers and bend your hand up at the wrist so that your palm is exposed.

KOKEN *(wrist joint)*

The hand bent down at the wrist and fingers extended. Strike with the top of the wrist.

HIRABASAMI

The index finger and thumb bent as if forming a letter "C" and the ring and pinky fingers folded at the second knuckles but without joining the palm of your hand. This technique is commonly used to strike the throat with the thenar space (the webbing area between your index and thumb) of your hand and grabbing or squeezing the windpipe afterwards.

YUBI BASAMI

The index finger and thumb bent as if forming a letter "C" while the rest of the finger are folded against the palm of your hand with the second knuckles sticking out. The second knuckle of your ring finger is used to strike the windpipe while the index finger and thumb are used grab and squeeze the windpipe.

HAITO

The hand and fingers completely extended and the thumb folded inward toward the palm. The side of the hand opposite to the pinky finger is used.

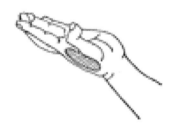

HAISHU

The hand and fingers completely extended and thumb folded against the palm. The back of the hand is used.

HIYI (elbow)

Elbow strikes are used to strike the chin, ribs, stomach or back of the head.

KOTE

The three areas of the forearm that are used are A) Omote, B) Era, C) Ura. This are commonly used to block.

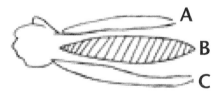

A
B
C

KA-SOKU-TEI

The heel. Normally used to kick behind or down.

SOKU-TO

The outer side of the foot. Used for side kicks.

YO-SOKU-TEI *(ball of the foot)*

The fingers raised completely to avoid injury, strike with the ball of the foot.

USHIRO-KAKA-TO

Back of the heel. Used for kicking back in a hook-like motion.

SOKO

The instep. Used to kick to the front or in a circular motion (round-house).

HIZA *(knee)*

An excellent weapon for close combat.

TACHIKATA
(STANCES)

HEISOKU-DACHI

Front

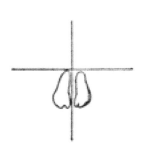

Feet together

Side

MUSUBI-DACHI

Front

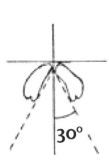

30°

Heels together with toes forming a 30° angle

Side

HEIKO-DACHI

Front

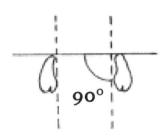

90°

Natural stance. Feet shoulder width apart and pointing forward.

Side

HACHIYI-DACHI

Front

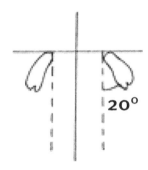

20°

Natural stance just as Heiko-Dachi but feet point outward forming a 20° angle

Side

NAI FAN CHIN-DACHI

Front

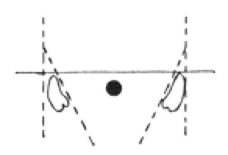

Stance simulating riding a horse. Feet wider than shoulders, pointing to the front and slighty inward.

Side

SHIKO-DACHI

Front

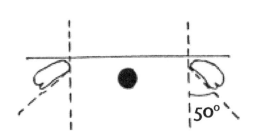

Side

This stance is similar to Nai Fan Chin-Dachi but feet and knees are pointed outward forming a 50° angle and the hips are lowered.

SANCHIN-DACHI

Front

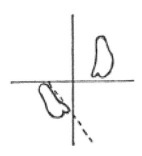

Side

The feet are shoulder width apart with the front foot heel positioned so that it creates a horizontal line with the toes of the other foot. The rear foot points to the front and the front foot points slightly inward. The whole body is tightened by contracting all muscles.

'T' YI-DACHI

Front

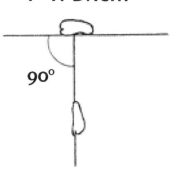

90°

Side

The rear foot points completely to the side of the body while the front foot points to the front forming a 90° angle. Both legs are slightly bent to be ready to move.

RENOYI-DACHI

Front

45°

Side

Natural position in which one foot points forward and the other one outward forming a 45° angle. Both legs are kept straight (no bend on the knees).

NEKO ASHI-DACHI

Front

30°

Side

Commonly referred as cat stance. The rear foot points outward in a 30° angle while the front leg rests on the ball of the foot putting most of the weight on the rear leg, knees are bent and the hip on the side of the rear foot is pushed out and the upper back is kept straight.

MOTO-DACHI

Front

Side

20°

Natural position as if stepping forward, the rear leg is kept straight while the other one is bent at the knee.

ZENKUTSU-DACHI

VIEW

Front

Side

The front leg is bent at the knee forming a vertical line with the toes, the rear leg is kept straight. While the front foot should be pointing forward, the rear foot is allowed to point slightly outward, approximately 30°. The hip should be kept at a 45° angle.

KOKUTSU-DACHI

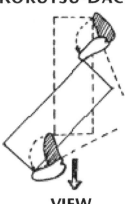

VIEW

Front

Side

The front leg is bent at the knee forming a vertical line with the toes and the rear leg is kept straight. While the front foot should be pointing forward the rear foot is allowed to point slightly outward, approximately 30°. This stance is exactly the same as Zenkutsu-Dachi except that the face is turned to the rear and the hips are turned further. This stance is mostly used for blocking and evasive techniques.

KOSA-DACHI

In this stance the feet are crossed, the front foot is firmly planted on the ground while the other one rests on the ball of the foot.

Front

Side

SAGI ASHI-DACHI

45°

In this stance the whole body rests on one leg while the other one is raised so that the foot is at knee height.

Saguiashi-Dachi
(Variations)

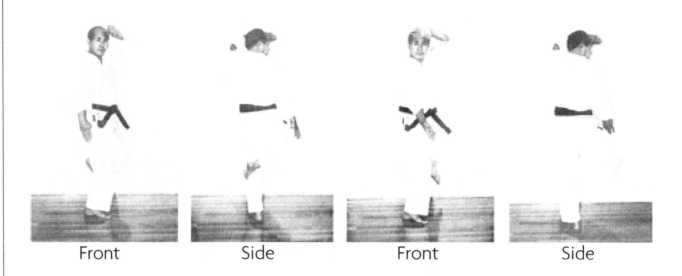

| Front | Side | Front | Side |

Uki Ashi-Dachi

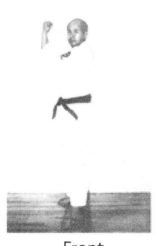

Front

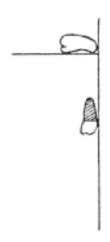

The rear foot is pointing completely to the side while the front foot is pointing forward with the heel slightly raised. Normally this stance is used to provoke an attack from the opponent.

Side

TSUKI
(STRIKES)

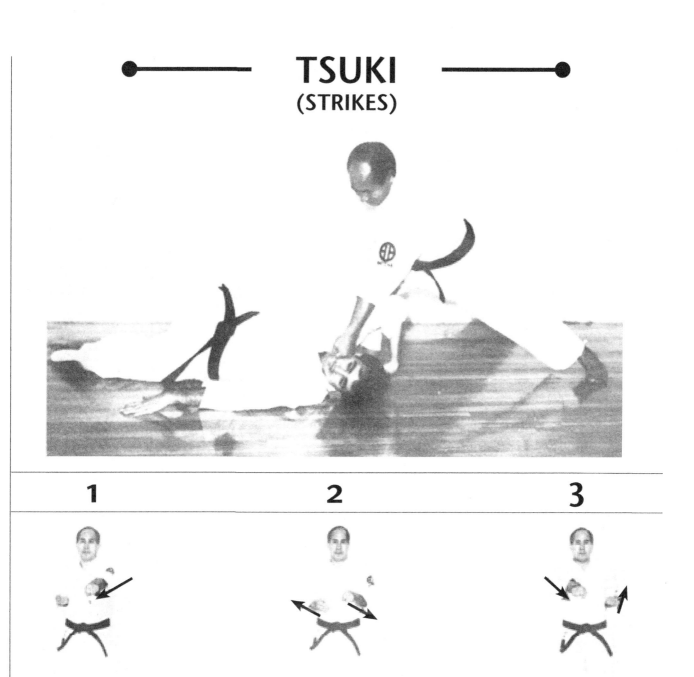

| 1 | 2 | 3 |

1. Standing in a practical striking stance, pull your right fist back so that your forearm is parallel to the floor and the palm of your hand is facing up, your fist and elbow should form a straight line. Extend your left arm with the palm of your hand facing down making a fist.

2. Pull your left arm back in a straight line towards the side of your body, simultaneously, extend your right arm throwing the fist forward in a straight line with as much speed and power as possible.

3. Your right arm should be completely extended with the palm of your hand facing down. Your shoulders shouldn't move and are kept relaxed and in their natural position throughout the movement.

OI-ZUKI

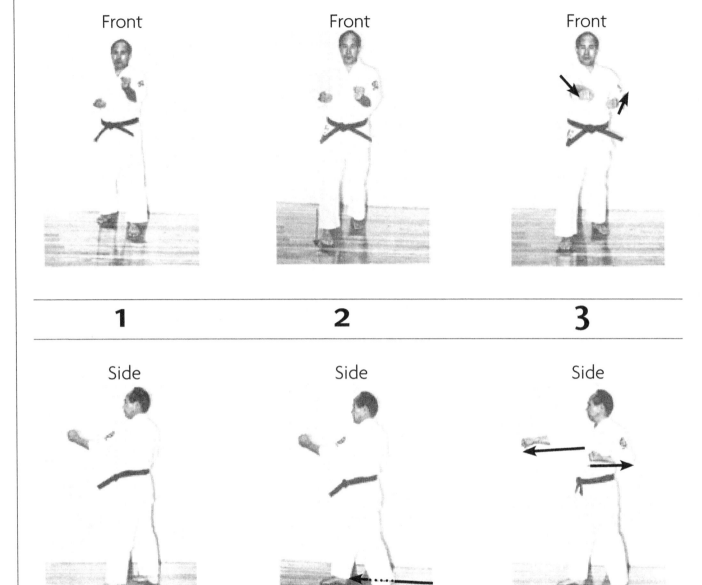

Front   Front   Front

1   **2**   **3**

Side   Side   Side

This striking technique is delivered by stepping forward. If stepping with the right foot, the right arm is used to strike, if stepping with the left foot, the left arm is used to strike.

1. Stand in Kamae (combat ready stance) with your left foot forward.

2. Step forward with your right foot.

3. Once your right foot is firmly planted on the ground throw your right fist forward to strike your opponent while simultaneously pulling your left fist toward the side of your body.

GYAKU ZUKI

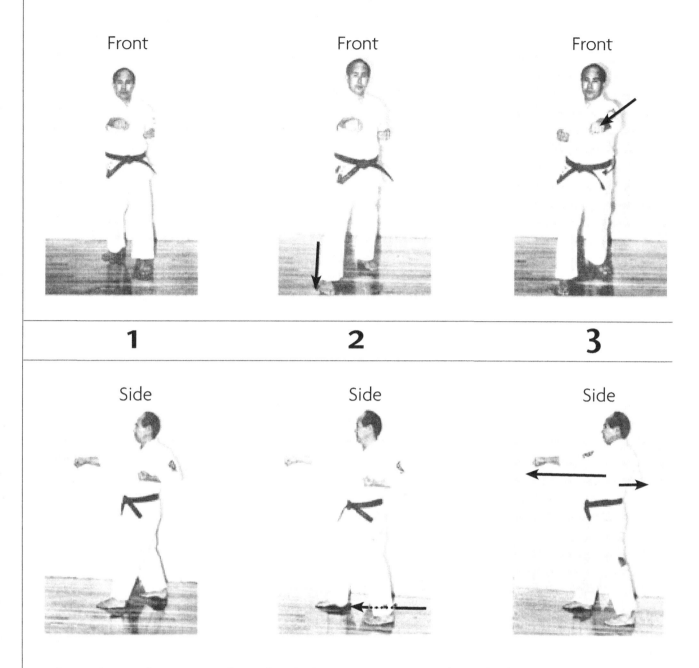

Front	Front	Front
1	**2**	**3**
Side	Side	Side

This striking technique is performed with the arm opposite in side to the leg, it can be done in a static position or stepping forward or backwards. If stepping with the right foot strike with the left fist and if stepping with the left foot strike with the right fist.

1. Stand in Kamae with your left foot forward, your right arm extended to the front of your body in Zuki form and your left arm pulled back to the side of your body.

2. Step forward with your right foot.

3. Once your right foot is firmly planted on the ground throw your left fist forward to strike your opponent while simultaneously pulling your right fist toward the side of your body. Power is added to this movement by rotating the hips toward the direction that the technique is executed.

MAETE ZUKI

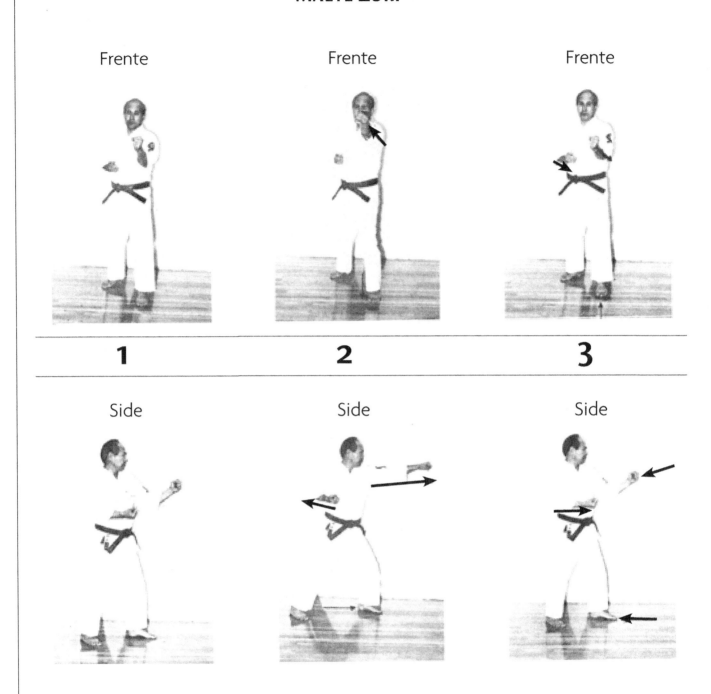

Frente   Frente   Frente

1   **2**   **3**

Side   Side   Side

This striking technique is done with the hand that is on the same side as the front foot, it can be done in a static position or moving forward without changing stance.

1. Stand in kamae with your left foot forward.

2. Slide your left foot forward while simultaneously throwing your left fist in the same direction and pulling your right arm back.

3. Return to kamae.

MOROTE ZUKI

Frente   Frente

1   **2**

Side   Side

1. Stand in kamae with your left foot forward and both fist pulled to your sides.

2. Throw your right fist forward toward the opponent's face while simultaneously throwing your left fist forward with the palm up toward the opponent's stomach. If your right foot is in front the left fist strikes the face and the right fist the stomach. This can also be applied with both fists parallel or both palms facing down.

FURI ZUKI

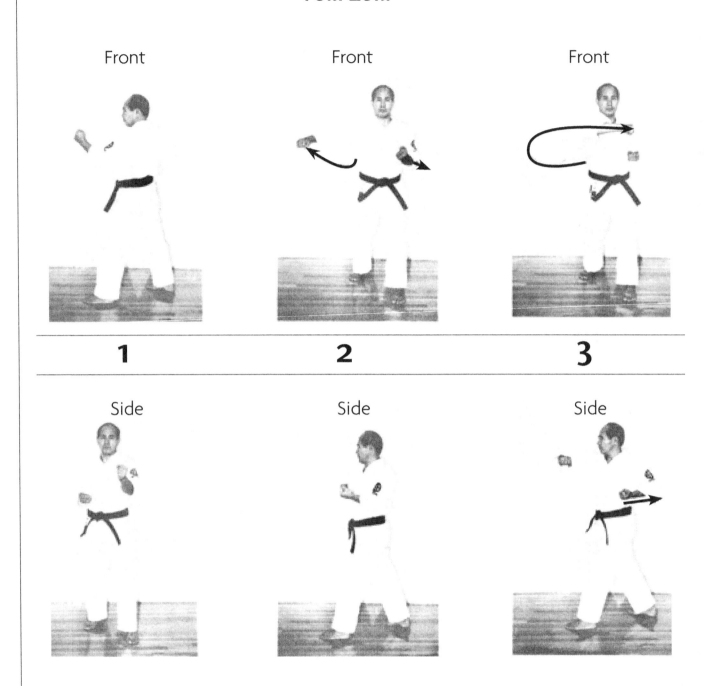

Front	Front	Front
1	**2**	**3**
Side	Side	Side

1. Stand in kamae with your right fist on the side of your body.

2. Swing your right arm away and to the front of your body.

3. Crossing it in a circular motion to strike the opponent in front of you in a hook-like motion.

KAGI ZUKI

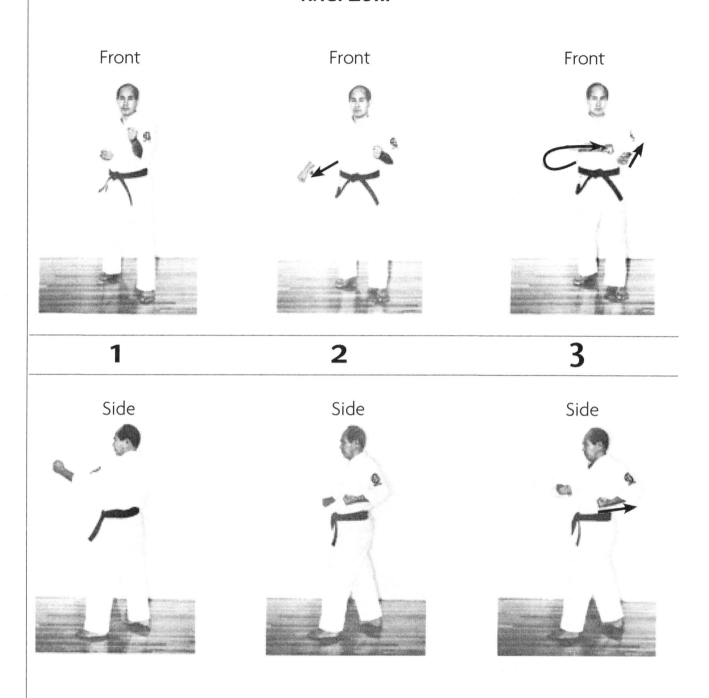

Front 1   Front 2   Front 3

Side   Side   Side

1. Stand in kamae with your right fist on the side of your body

2. guide your right fist away and to the side of your body.

3. Throw your right fist as straight as possible toward your left side while simultaneously pulling your left fist toward the side of your body, the striking arm should stop only when the forearm and arm form a 90° angle.

URA ZUKI

Front · · · · · · · · · · · · Front

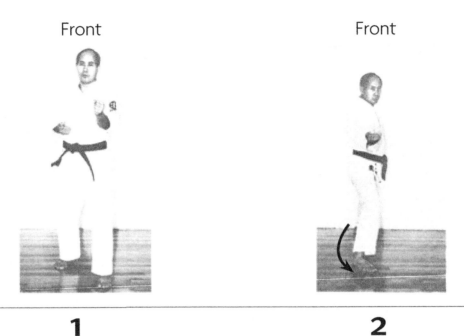

1 · · · · · · · · · · · · **2**

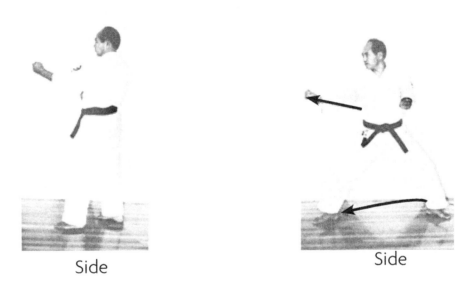

Side · · · · · · · · · · · · Side

1. Stand in kamae with your right fist in front of your solar plexus.

2. Step forward with your right foot placing it in a straight line with your left foot and turning your body sideways to end in a Shiko-Dachi stance and throw your right fist away and up from the side of your body with the palm facing up towards your opponent's solar plexus while simultaneously pulling your left fist back toward the side of your body.

Age Zuki

Front · 1

Front · 2

Front · 3

Side

Side

Side

1. Stand in kamae.

2. Step with your right foot forward to end in a Shiko-Dachi stance.

3. Simultaneously throw your right fist up and forward to strike your opponent's chin.

UCHI

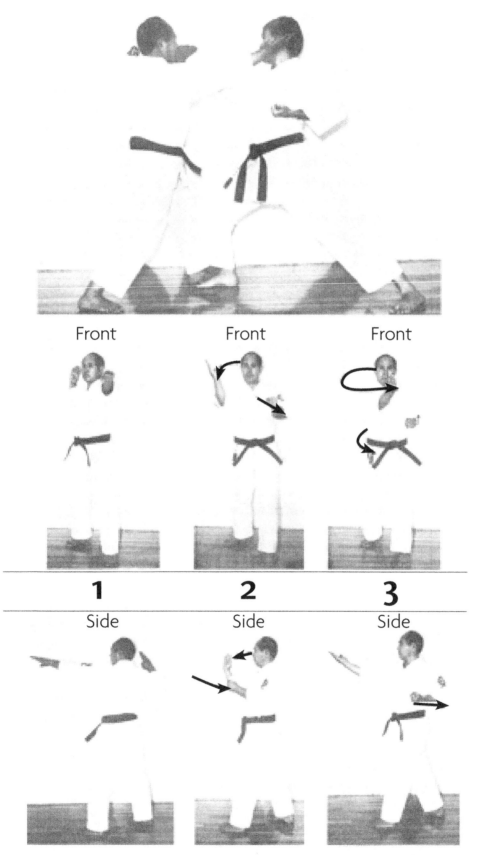

Front   Front   Front

1   **2**   **3**

Side   Side   Side

SHUTO UCHI

1. Stand in kamae and extend your left arm to the front of your body with an open hand, palm facing down, place your right hand open and pointing up close to your right ear.

2. Throw your right arm forward in a circular motion while simultaneously pulling your left arm back so that your fist is at the side of your body.

3. The technique ends with your right palm facing up and your left fist pulled back ready to strike. The outer edge of the hand (Shuto) is used to strike in this technique.

URA UCHI

This technique uses the back of the fist and there are two variations;

MAE URA UCHI

1. Standing in a natural position place both arms in front of your body with closed fists in front of your shoulders, your arms forming a 90º angle with the elbows close (about 3 inches) to your ribcage. The palms of your hands facing you.

2. Extend your left arm to the front of your body throwing your fist forward in a whip-like motion toward the opponent face.

3. Return the left fist to its initial position. Throughout the movement the right arm stays in the same position.

Front	Front	Front
1	**2**	**3**
Side	Side	Side

YOKO URA UCHI

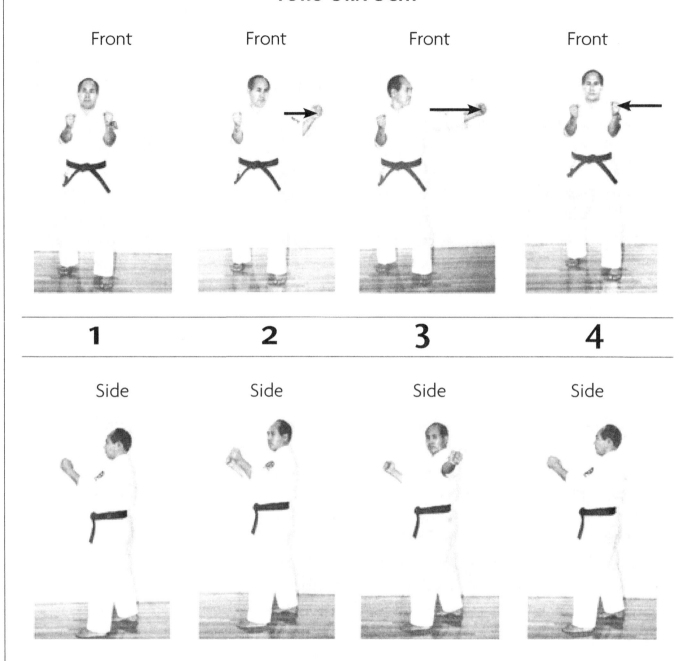

1   2   3   4

1. Standing in a natural position place both arms in front of your body with closed fists in front of your shoulders, your arms forming a 90º angle, with the elbows close (about 3 inches) to your ribcage. The palms of your hands facing each other.

2. Extend your left arm to the side of your body

3. throwing your fist in a whip-like motion and hitting your opponent in the face with the back of the first two knuckles of your hand (Ura Ken).

4. Return the left fist to its initial position. Throughout the movement the right arm stays in the same position. The hip is turned a little at the moment of impact to add more power.

HAITO UCHI

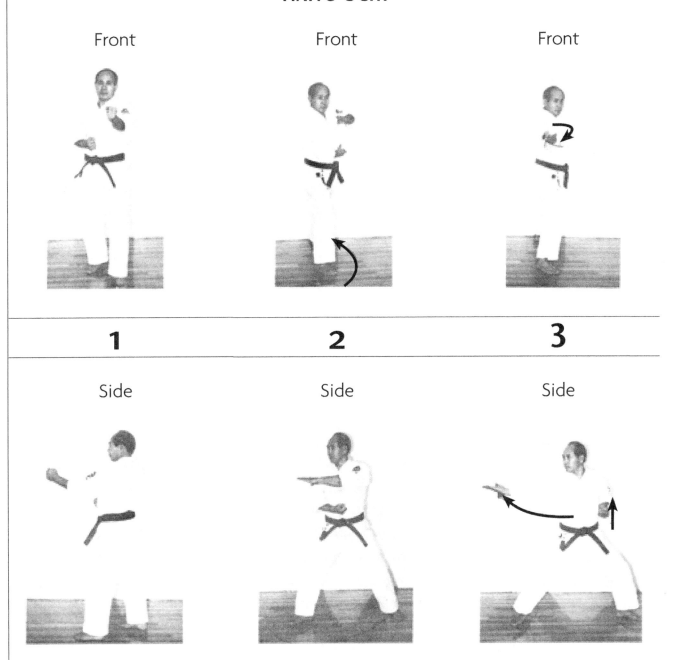

Front   Front   Front

1   **2**   **3**

Side   Side   Side

This technique is performed with an open hand. The hand and fingers completely extended and the thumb folded inward toward the palm. The side of the hand opposite to the pinky finger is used (Haito).

1. Stand in Kamae.

2. Step back with your left foot placing it in a straight line with the right foot and turning your body sideways to end in a Shiko-Dachi stance.

3. Throw your right hand with the palm facing up to the side of your body to strike the oponent with the side of your hand (Haito), simultaneously pull your left arm to the side of your body.

HAITO UCHI
(variant)

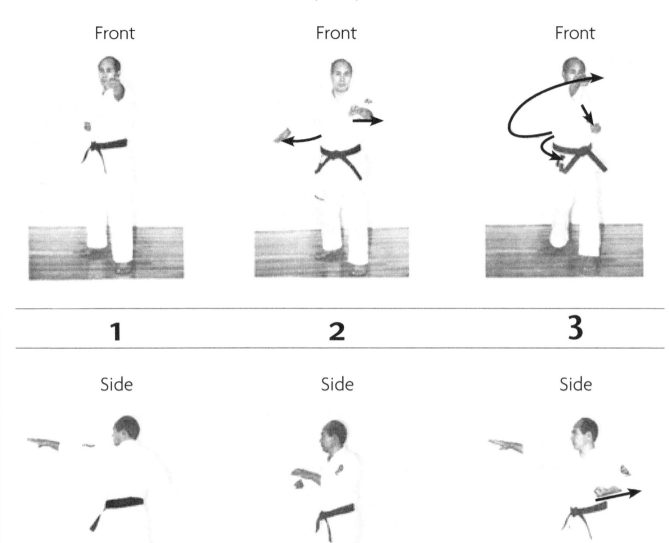

Front   Front   Front

1   **2**   **3**

Side   Side   Side

1. Stand in kamae.

2. Throw your open right hand forward in a semicircular motion with the palm facing down and turn you hip to add power to the technique.

3. Simultaneously pull your left fist to the side of your body.

KEN TSUI UCHI

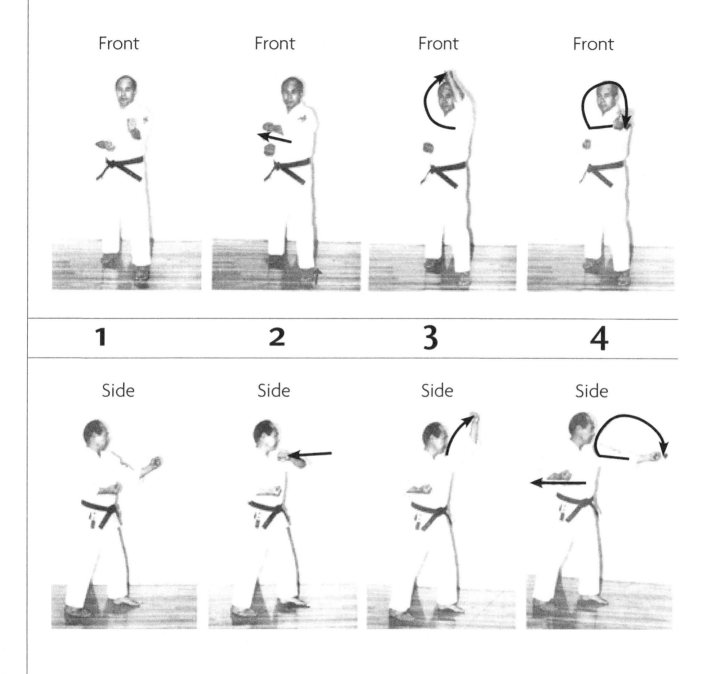

Front   Front   Front   Front

1   2   3   4

Side   Side   Side   Side

1. Stand in kamae.

2. Bend your left elbow toward your right shoulder.

3. Move your left fist up in a circular motion.

4. Throw your left fist down to strike with the outer edge of your fist.

ATE

HIJI ATE

Elbow strikes. There are five variations; Tate, Mawashi, Yoko, Otoshi and Ushiro.

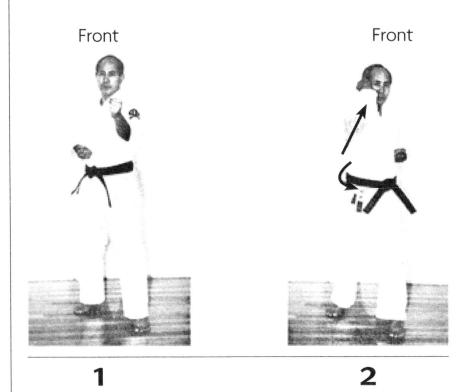

Front

Front

1

2

TATE HIJI ATE

1. Stand in kamae.

2. Throw your right elbow up and turn your hip until your fist is positioned next to your ear, palm facing you, simultaneously pull your left fist back to the side of your body.

Front

Front

MAWASHI HIJI ATE

1. Stand in kamae.

2. Throw your right elbow forward and turn your hip until your fist is positioned in front of your chest, simultaneously pull your left fist back to the side of your body.

YOKO HIJI ATE

1	2	3
Front	Front	Front

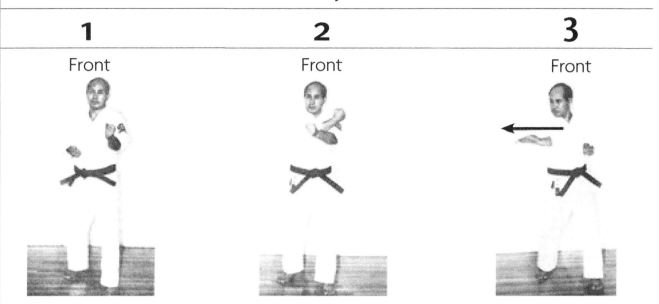

1. Stand in kamae.

2. Cross your right arm in front of your body until your fist is on top of your left shoulder while trying to keep your fist as close as possible to your body.

3. Throw your right elbow out to the side of your body, simultaneously pull your left fist back.

OTOSHI HIJI ATE

1	2	3
Front	Front	Front

1. Stand in kamae.

2. Extend your right arm up so that your fist is on top of your head.

3. Throw your right elbow down and turn your hip to add more power, at the same time pull your left fist back to the side of your body.

Ushiro Hiji Ate

1	**2**	**3**
Front	Front	Front

1. Stand in kamae.

2. Extend your right arm forward, palm facing down.

3. Throw your elbow back turning the wrist so that the palm is facing up at the side of your body. Try to keep your arm as close as possible to your body.

Hiza Ate

1	**2**	**3**
Front	Front	Front

1. Stand in kamae.

2. Throw your right knee forward and up. Your left foot should be well grounded on the floor throughout the technique.

3. Return your right foot to its initial position.

KERI

MAE GERI

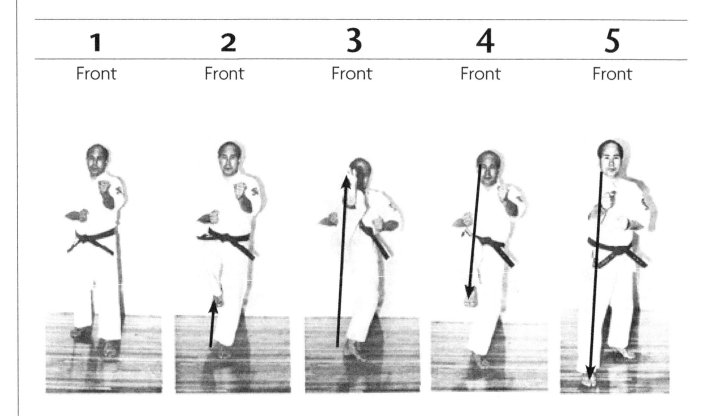

1. Stand in kamae.

2. Raise your right knee until your right foot is parallel to your left knee.

3. Throw your right foot forward by extending your knee and pull your toes back to strike with the ball of the foot (Yo-Soku-Tei), at the same time pull your right fist back. Your left foot should be kept firmly grounded throughout the technique and your body kept straight.

4. After impact your foot should return immediately to the side of your knee.

5. Return your foot to its initial position.

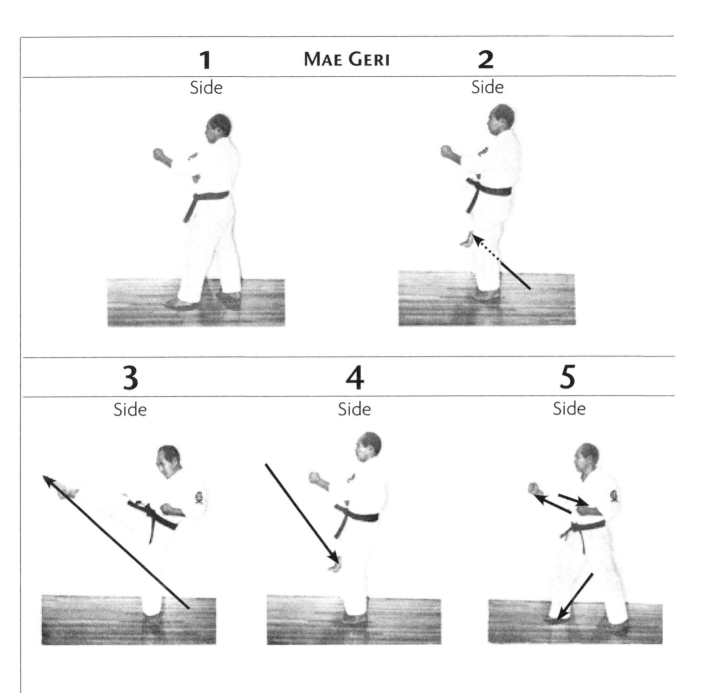

1	2
Side	Side

3	4	5
Side	Side	Side

OI GERI

This technique is exactly the same as Mae Geri with the exception that after the kick is performed the foot returns to the side of the left knee and then forward as if stepping.

HIKI GERI

This kick is performed in a whip-like motion with the front or back foot following the same technique as Mae Geri and returning the foot to its initial position.

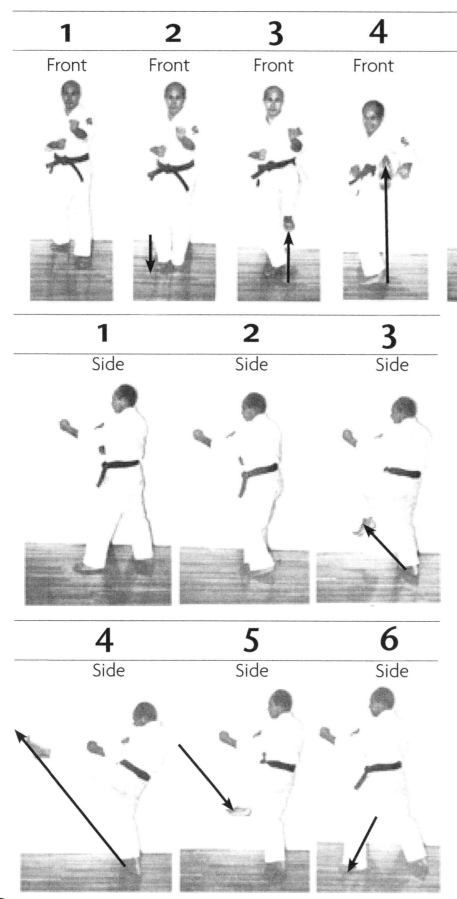

1. Stand in kamae.

2. Quickly join your right foot with your left one.

3. Lift your left knee so that your foot is parallel to your right knee.

4. Throw your left foot forward by extending your knee and pull your toes back to strike with the ball of the foot (Yo-Soku-Tei), at the same time pull your left fist back. Your right foot should be kept firmly grounded throughout the technique and your body kept straight.

5. After impact immediately flex your knee back.

6. Place your foot on the ground.

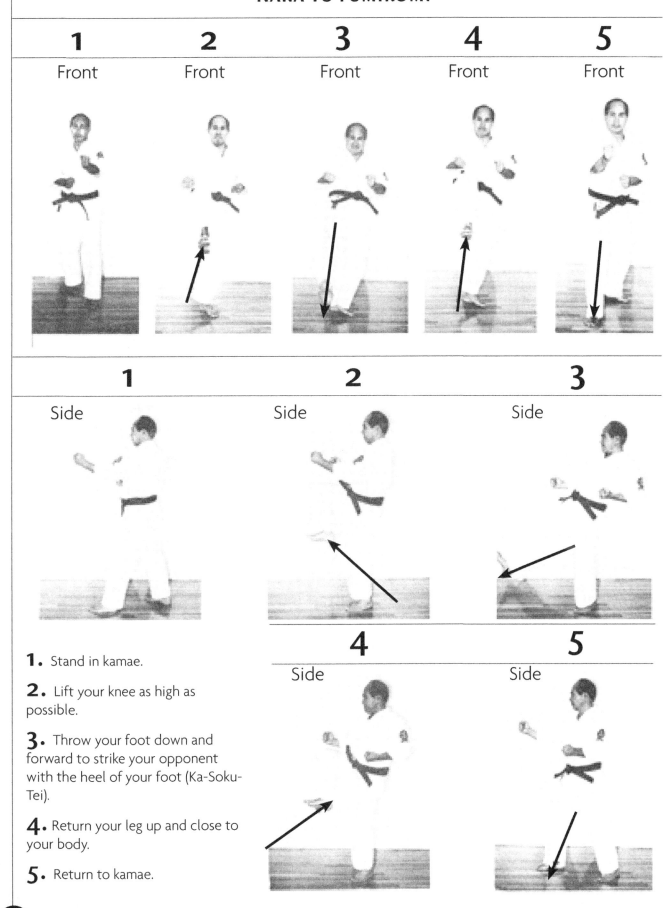

1. Stand in kamae.

2. Lift your knee as high as possible.

3. Throw your foot down and forward to strike your opponent with the heel of your foot (Ka-Soku-Tei).

4. Return your leg up and close to your body.

5. Return to kamae.

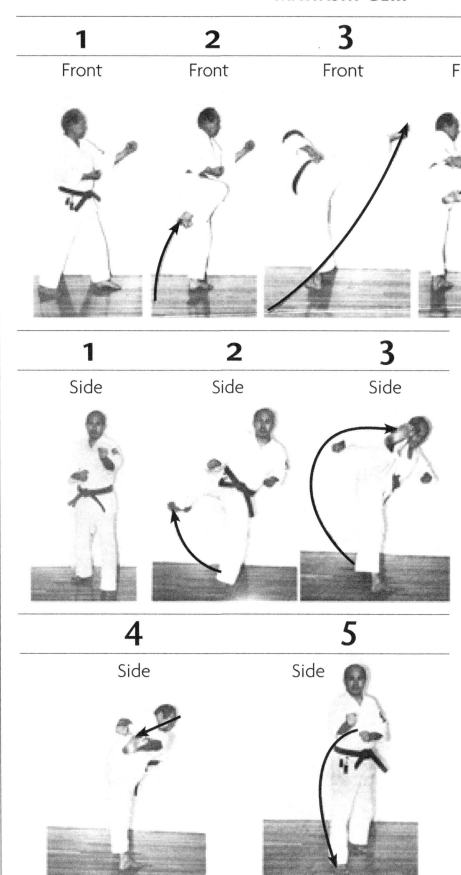

1	2	3	4	5
Front	Front	Front	Front	Front

1	2	3
Side	Side	Side

4	5
Side	Side

1. Stand in kamae.

2. Raise your right leg to your side and up until it is perpendicular to your body.

3. Throw your foot forward in a circular motion to strike with the ball of the foot (Yo Soku-Tei) or with the instep (soko), at the same time turn your hip forward.

4. After impact immediately return your leg to the side of your body by flexing your knee.

5. Place your foot on the ground and stand in kamae.

1	2	3	4	5	6
Front	Front	Front	Front	Front	Front

1	2	3
Side	Side	Side

4	5	6
Side	Side	Side

1. Stand in a natural position and place your left fist in front of your solar plexus and your right arm semi-extended to your side, the fist placed at shoulder height, turning your head to look to your right side.

2. Step sideways by crossing your left foot in front of your right one and placing it at its side.

3. Lift your right knee up in front of your body so that the foot is parallel to your left knee.

4. Throw the right foot to your side by extending the knee to strike with the outer edge of your foot (Soku-To) and pause for a moment after impact. Turn the hip in the direction of the kick to add power to it.

5. Return your knee to the front of your body.

6. Place your foot back on the ground in front of you.

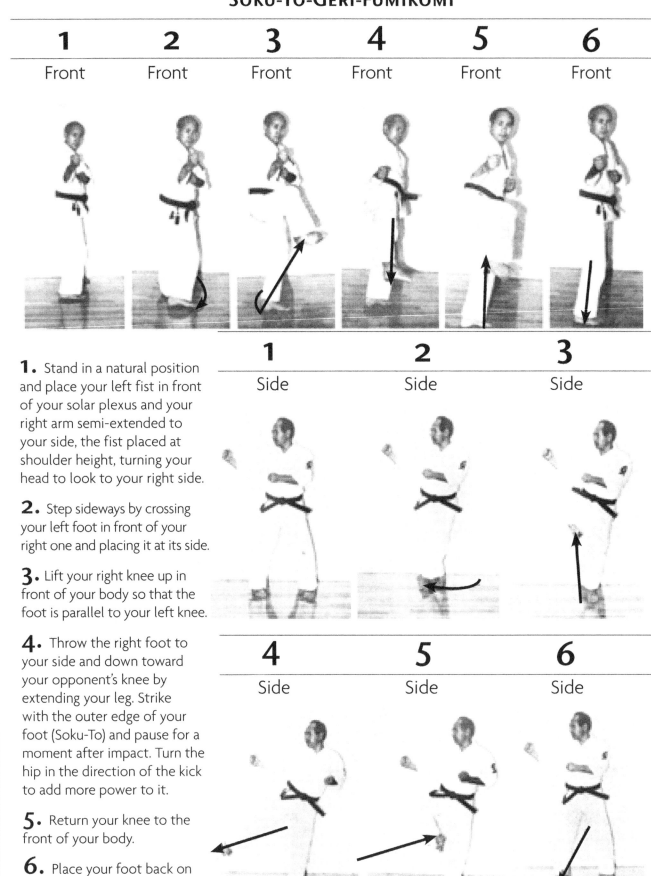

1. Stand in a natural position and place your left fist in front of your solar plexus and your right arm semi-extended to your side, the fist placed at shoulder height, turning your head to look to your right side.

2. Step sideways by crossing your left foot in front of your right one and placing it at its side.

3. Lift your right knee up in front of your body so that the foot is parallel to your left knee.

4. Throw the right foot to your side and down toward your opponent's knee by extending your leg. Strike with the outer edge of your foot (Soku-To) and pause for a moment after impact. Turn the hip in the direction of the kick to add more power to it.

5. Return your knee to the front of your body.

6. Place your foot back on the ground in front of you.

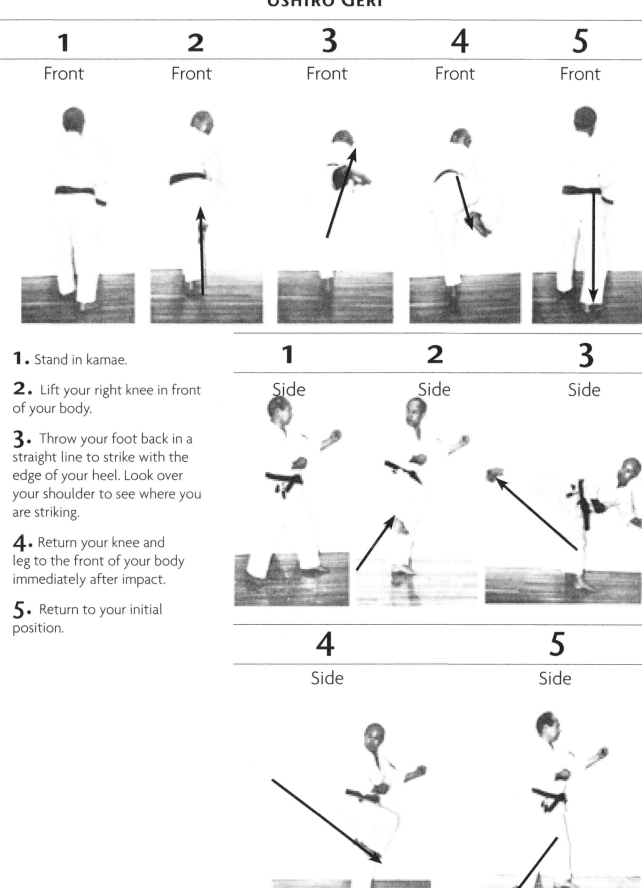

1	2	3	4	5
Front	Front	Front	Front	Front

1	2	3
Side	Side	Side

4	5
Side	Side

1. Stand in kamae.

2. Lift your right knee in front of your body.

3. Throw your foot back in a straight line to strike with the edge of your heel. Look over your shoulder to see where you are striking.

4. Return your knee and leg to the front of your body immediately after impact.

5. Return to your initial position.

NIDAN-GERI

1. Stand in kamae.

2. Jump up and forward and throw your right foot forward to strike with the ball of the foot (Yo-Soku-Tei).

3. After impact immediately return the right foot and throw the left one in the same way.

4. After impact return your left foot immediately.

5. Land on the ground standing in kamae.

YOKO TOBI GERI

1. Stand in kamae.

2. jump forward and up and turn your body so that your opponent is at your right side

3. Bend your left leg so that you foot is parallel to your right knee and extend your right leg to strike with the outer edge of the foot (Soku-To)

4. After impact return your feet to land standing in kamae

UKE
(BLOCKING)

AGUE UKE

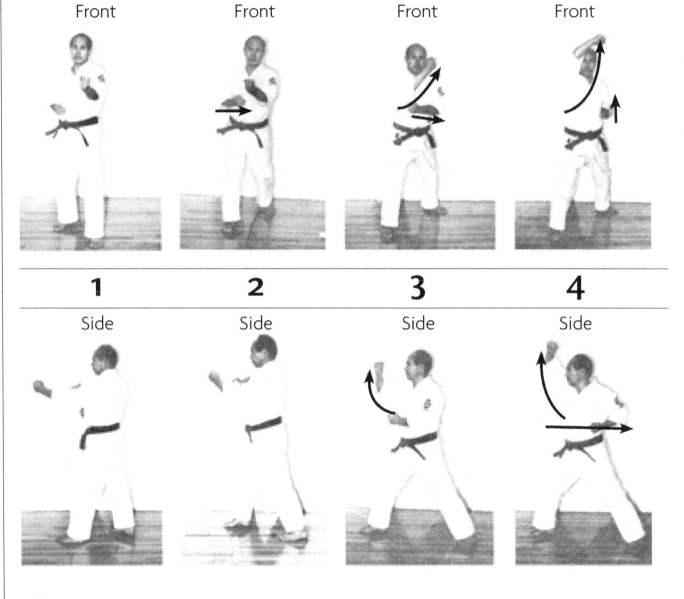

Front · Front · Front · Front

1 · **2** · **3** · **4**

Side · Side · Side · Side

1. Stand in kamae.

2. Step back.

3. Raise your right forearm and cross it in front of your head to block a strike directed to your face, at the same time pull your left arm back to the side of your body.

4. This technique ends with the right forearm above and slightly in front of your head. The fist goes above the elbow forming a 45 angle in relation to the line of your body.

Application

UCHI UKE

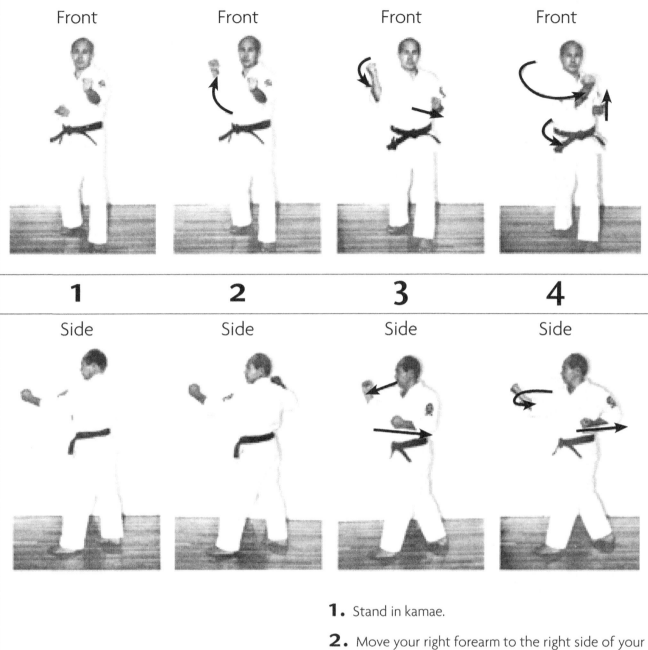

Front   Front   Front   Front

1   **2**   **3**   **4**

Side   Side   Side   Side

1. Stand in kamae.

2. Move your right forearm to the right side of your body with the fist pointing up.

3. Swing your right forearm to block a strike directed to you solar plexus or chest, simultaneously pull your left arm back to the side of your body.

4. The right forearm continues until the fist is in front of the left shoulder, palm facing you.

Application

SOTO UKE

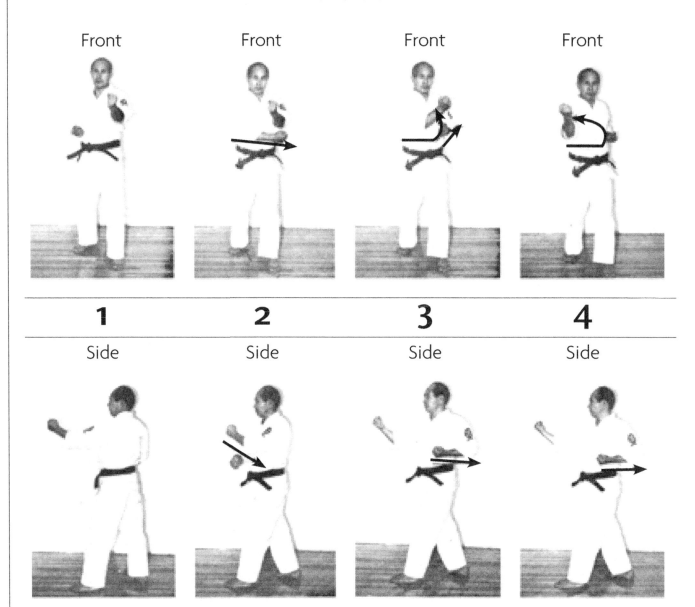

Front   Front   Front   Front

1   **2**   **3**   **4**

Side   Side   Side   Side

1. Stand in kamae.

2. Move your right forearm to the front of your body so that your fist is below your left arm.

3. Pivoting on the elbow, swing your right fist up and to the right.

4. Finish this technique with your right fist directly in front of your shoulder, fist pointing up and elbow down close to your body, palm facing you.

Application

Jiyi Sasae Uke

Front   Front   Front   Front

1   **2**   **3**   **4**

Side   Side   Side   Side

1. Stand in kamae.

2. Step back and move your right forearm to the front of your body so that your fist is below your left arm.

3. Pivoting on the elbow, swing your right fist up and to the right, simultaneously place your left fist at the side of your elbow to support your arm against a powerful attack. The hip is turned to the opposite side in which the block was performed.

4. Finish this technique with your right fist directly in front of your shoulder, fist pointing up and elbow down close to your body, palm facing you and your left fist supporting your right elbow.

Application

Same as the previous one (Hiji Sasae Uke) with the exception that the left hand is supporting the right arm by placing your open hand against your right wrist.

Application

HARAI UKE
(GEDAN BARAI UKE)

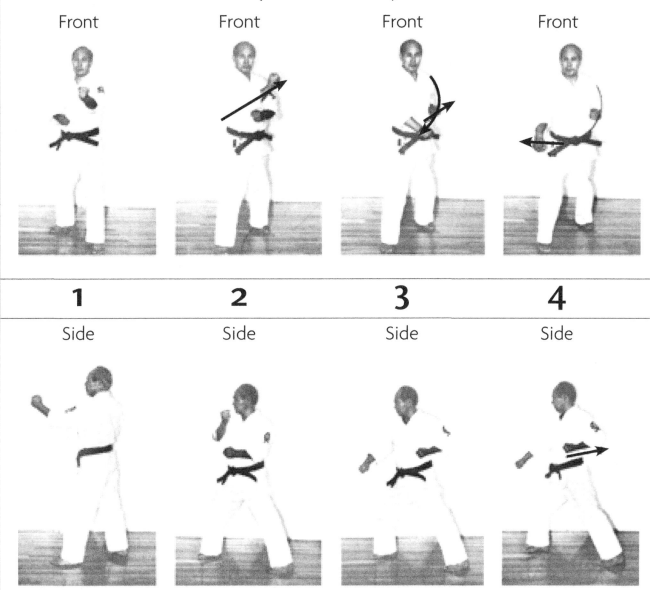

Front   Front   Front   Front

1   **2**   **3**   **4**

Side   Side   Side   Side

1. Stand in kamae.

2. Step back and cross your right arm in front of your body so that your fist is in front of your left bicep.

3. Swing your right forearm down and to your right to block a low blow or kick, simultaneously pull your left arm back to the side of your body and rotate your hip to the opposite side of the block.

4. Finish this technique with your right arm extended above and parallel to your right leg and the left arm pulled back to the side of your body.

Application

KOSA UKE

This technique is performed by crossing the forearms and it can be done with open or closed hands. Two variants exist; Yodan Kosa Uke and Gedan Kosa Uke.

YODAN KOSA UKE

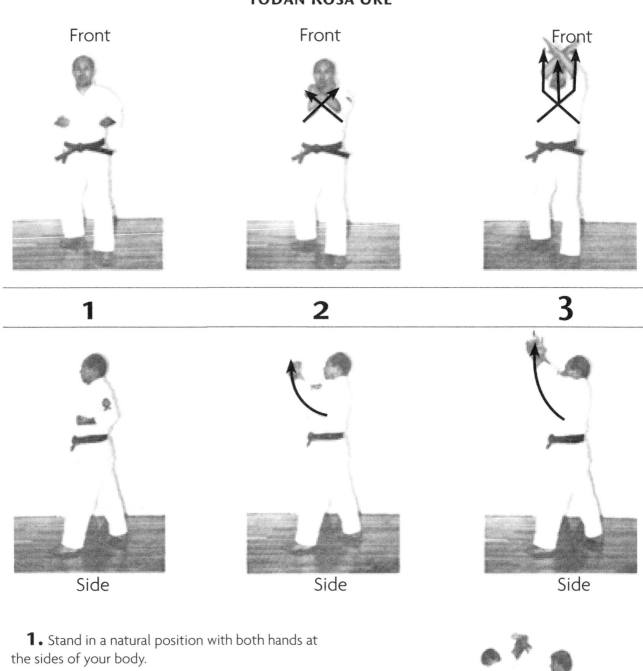

Front   Front   Front

1   **2**   **3**

Side   Side   Side

1. Stand in a natural position with both hands at the sides of your body.

2. Move both hands up and to the front of your body crossing your forearms to block against a blow to the face.

3. This technique is finished when your hands are above and slightly in front of your head.

Application

GEDAN KOSA UKE

Front   Front   Front

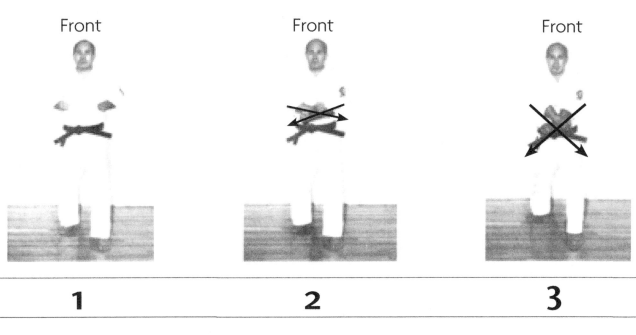

1   2   3

Side

Side

Side

1. Stand in a natural position with both hands at the sides of your body.

2. Move both hands down and to the front of your body crossing your forearms to block against a low blow or kick.

3. This technique is finished when your arms are completely extended and parallel to the front leg.

Application

Kakiwake Uke

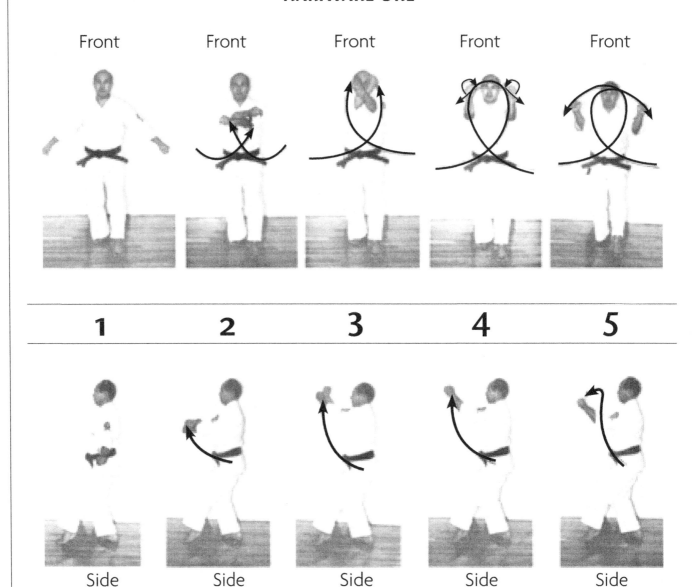

Front	Front	Front	Front	Front
1	**2**	**3**	**4**	**5**
Side	Side	Side	Side	Side

1. Stand in Neko-Ashi-Dachi with both arms extended down and to your sides.

2. Move your arms to the front of your shoulders crossing them.

3. Raise your arms in front of your face with the palms of your hands facing you.

4. Separate your arms to your sides rotating your fists so that the palms of your hands face away.

5. Continue until your wrist form a line with the outside of your shoulders and are at shoulder height.

Application

NAGASHI UKE

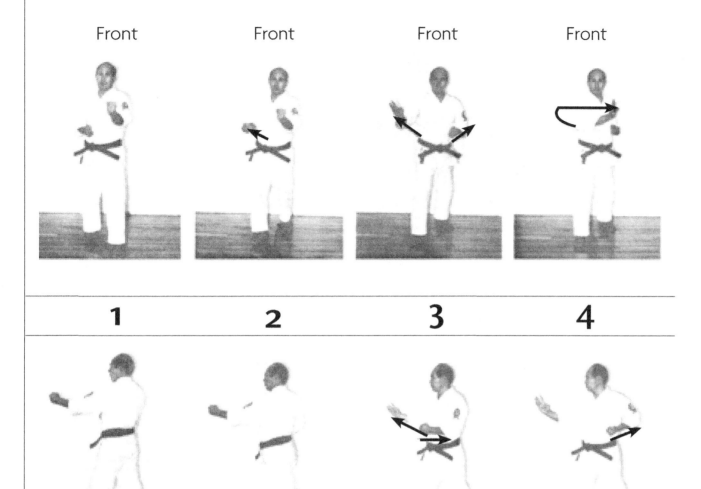

Front	Front	Front	Front
1	**2**	**3**	**4**
Side	Side	Side	Side

1. Stand in kamae.

2. Step back.

3. Cross your right open hand in front of your body to deflect a strike, simultaneously pull your left arm to the side of your body.

4. Deflect the opponent's strike by meeting him at his forearm and continue until his strike is outside the line of your body. If the strike is aimed at the head this technique would be called Yodan-Nagashi-Uke, if it is aimed at the chest it would be called Shudan-Nagashi-Uke.

Application

GEDAN NAGASHI UKE

Front | Front | Front

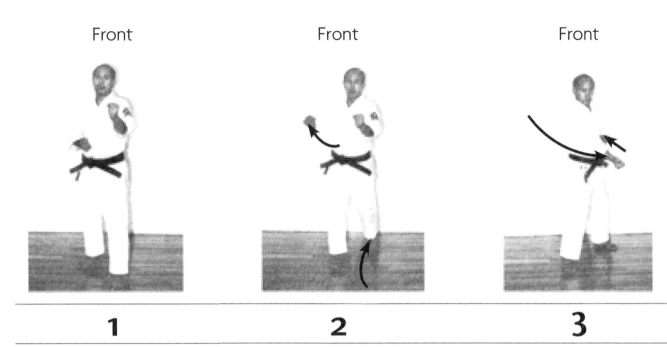

1   **2**   **3**

Side   Side   Side

1. Stand in kamae.

2. Step back.

3. Extend your right arm down and cross it through the front of your body with the palm of your hand facing your opponent, simultaneously rotate your hip toward the direction of the block and pull your left arm to the side of your body. Continue until your opponent's kick is outside of the line of your body.

Application

SUSKUI UKE

Front | Front | Front

1   **2**   **3**

Side | Side | Side

1. Stand in kamae.

2. Open your right hand and move it forward and up in a circular motion with the palm of your hand facing up.

3. Intercept your opponent's arm by placing your hand below his elbow and pushing his arm up, simultaneously pull your left arm to the side of your body or place it in front of your forehead with the palm of your hand facing away.

Application

SHUTO UKE

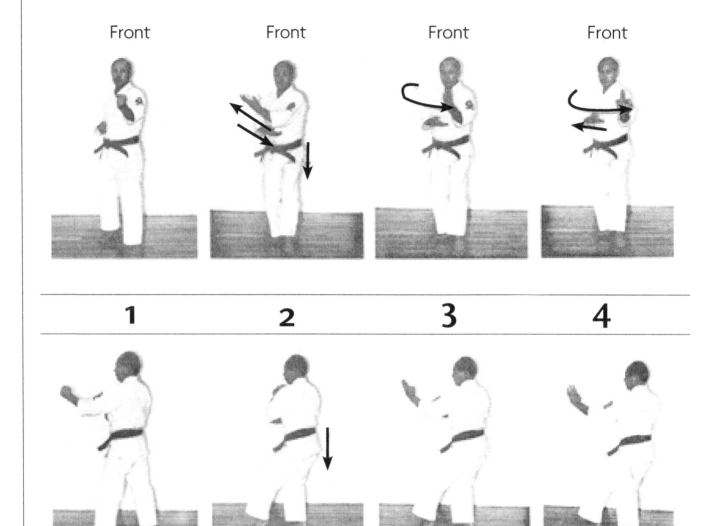

Front Front Front Front

1 **2** **3** **4**

Side Side Side Side

Application

1. Stand in kamae

2. Drop to Neko-Ashi-Dachi and move your open left hand to the right side of your body in front of your bicep.

3. Quickly swing your left hand to the left side of your body and rotate your wrist, simultaneously, pull your right arm and place it in front of your solar plexus.

4. The outer edge of the hand is utilized to block the opponent's blow and pushing it to the outside of your body's line. This blocking technique is finalized with your left elbow pointing down and close to your body, your fingers pointing up and your right hand in front of your solar plexus with your palm facing up.

KAKETE UKE
(Naha-Te)

Front	Front	Front	Front
1	**2**	**3**	**4**

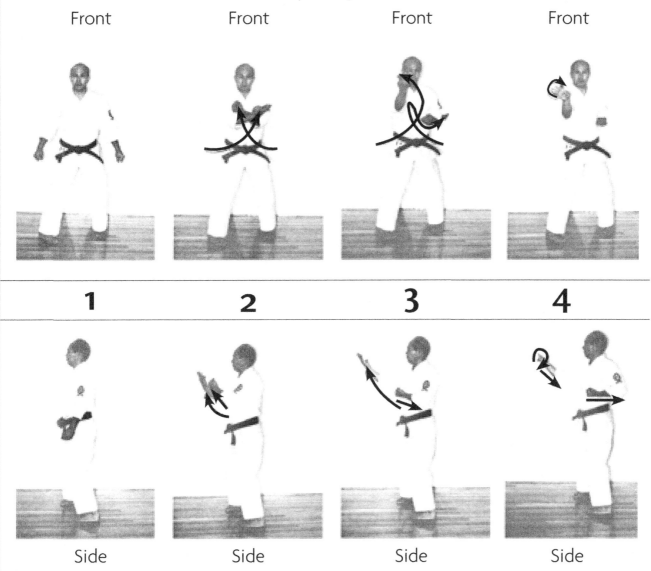

Side	Side	Side	Side

1. Stand in Sanchin-Dachi and extend your arms down and to the sides of your body.

2. Bring both hands close to your body in front of your chest in a circular motion and cross them with the right arm in front of the left one.

3. Pull your left arm to the side of your body and continue to move the right arm in a circular motion to the outside of your body with the palm of your hand facing you to first block the strike.

4. Rotate your wrist so that your palm is facing away from you. By now your left arm should be at the side of your body.

Application

KAKETE UKE
(Shuri-Te)

Front   Front   Front   Front

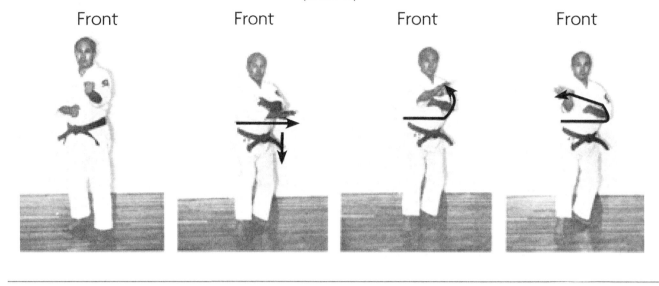

1   **2**   **3**   **4**

Side   Side   Side   Side

Application

1. Stand in kamae.

2. Step back and drop to Neko-Ashi-Dachi, simultaneously open your right hand and move it to your left side below your left elbow.

3. Move your right hand to your right side making small circular motion and bend your wrist to your right to block a blow aimed at your solar plexus.

4. Pull your right hand a little toward your body and place your left hand palm facing down in front of your solar plexus.

OSAE UKE

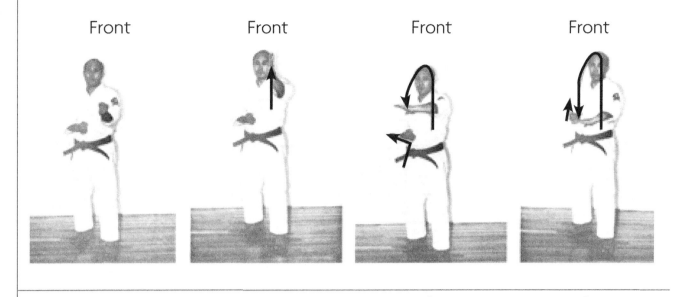

Front   Front   Front   Front

1   **2**   **3**   **4**

Side   Side   Side   Side

1. Stand in kamae.

2. Open your left hand and move it closer to your body.

3. Pivoting on your elbow move your hand down and pull your right arm to the side of your body.

4. Block the strike with the palm of your hand and push it down and out in a circular motion.

Application

Hiji Kuri Uke

Front   Front   Front   Front

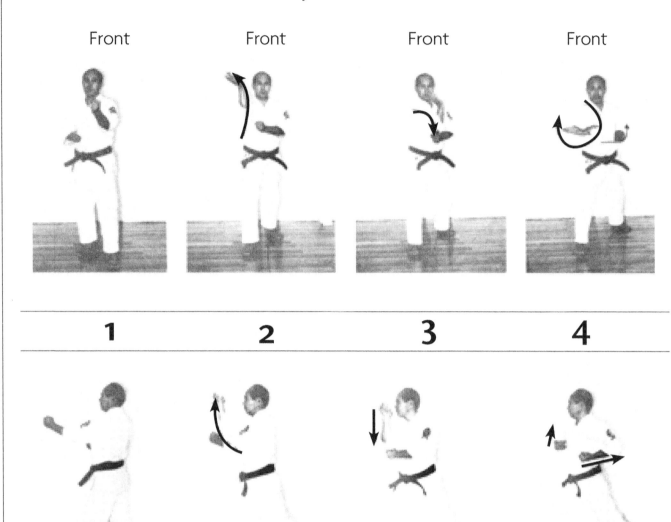

1   **2**   **3**   **4**

Side   Side   Side   Side

1. Stand in kamae.

2. Step back and raise your right arm.

3. Align your forearm with the centerline of your body. You can use an open hand or closed fist.

4. In a circular motion move your elbow to your right side deflecting your opponent's strike with your arm, simultaneously pull your left arm to the side of your body.

Application

NINO UDE UKE

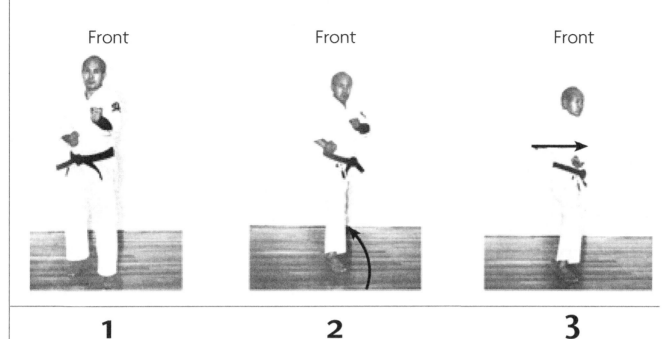

Front Front Front

1 **2** **3**

Side Side Side

1. Stand in kamae

2. Step back into Shiko-Dachi and move your right fist to your hip.

3. With your right fist on your hip swing your elbow in a straight line to the front of your body deflecting with your elbow your opponent's blow.

Application

SHIUKO UKE
(HAISHU)

Front   Front   Front   Front

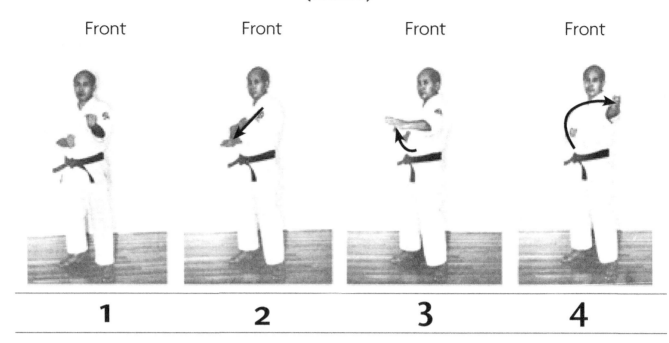

1   **2**   **3**   **4**

Side   Side   Side   Side

Application

1. Stand in kamae.

2. Open your left fist.

3. Move your left arm forward and to your left to intercept and deflect your opponent's blow, simultaneously pull your right arm to the side of your body.

4. Rotate your hips to add more power to the movement.

KO UKE

Front

Front

Front

1   **2**   **3**

Side

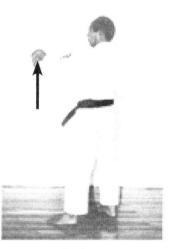

Side

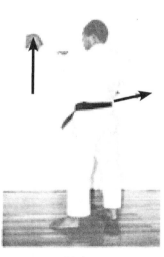

Side

1. Stand in kamae.

2. Raise your left wrist pointing your fingers down

3. Intercept your opponent's blow with your wrist and move it up until your hand is at the same height as your head, simultaneously pull your right arm to the side of your body. This blocking technique can also be performed to the side.

Application

Tsuki Uke

Front   Front

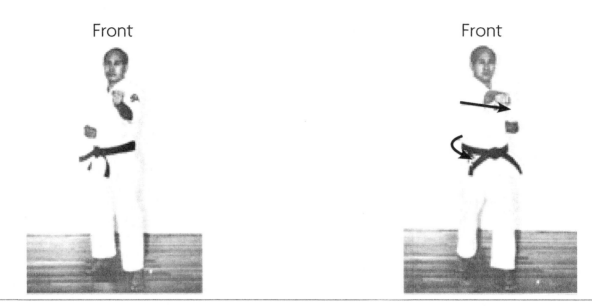

1   **2**

Side

Side

1. Stand in kamae

2. Throw your right arm in a straight line toward your opponent's solar plexus so that your arm goes below his in his attempt to strike you. You block his blow with your arm and you strike his solar plexus at the same time. Turn your hip and pull your left arm to the side of your body.

Application

UCHI OTOSHI UKE

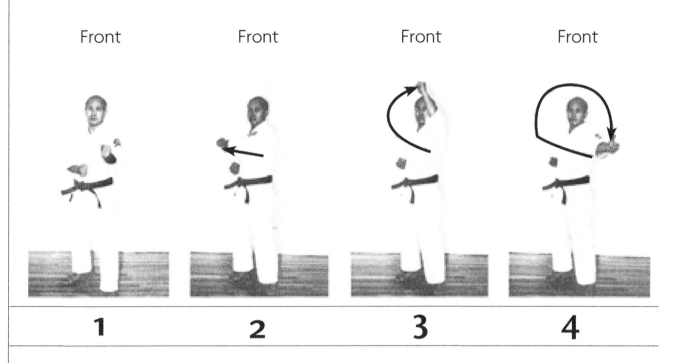

Front | Front | Front | Front

1   2   3   4

Side | Side | Side | Side

1. Stand in kamae.

2. Pull your left foot back and move your left arm to your right side.

3. In a circular motion move your left arm up.

4. Continue to move your left arm in a circular motion down and to the outside of your body mostly pivoting on your elbow to intercept and deflect your opponent's blow. After deflecting your opponent's blow your left arm should be completely extended and your right arm at the side of your body.

Application

YOKO BARAI UKE

Front	Front	Front	Front

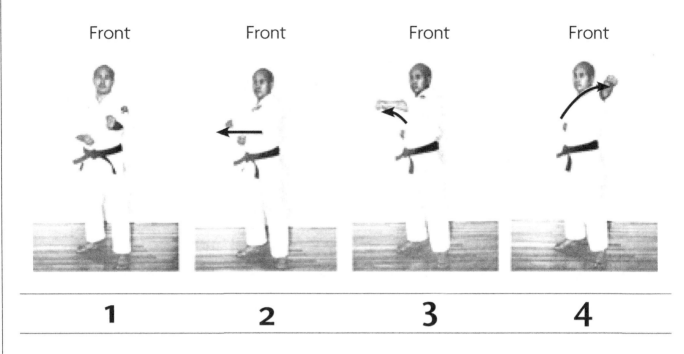

1	**2**	**3**	**4**

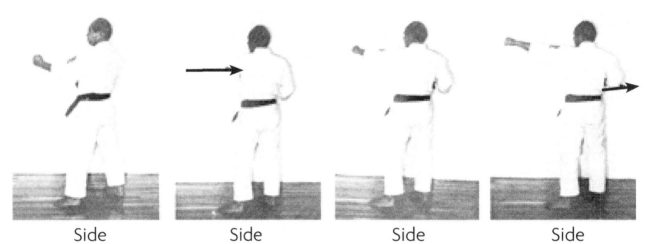

Side	Side	Side	Side

1. Stand in kamae.

2. Pull your left foot back and move your left arm to the right side of your body by bending your elbow so that your arm and forearm form a 90° angle.

3. Move your left arm to your left side in a straight line and pull your right arm to the side of your body.

4. With your closed fist palm facing down intercept your opponent's blow and move it away from your body.

Application

MAWASHI UKE

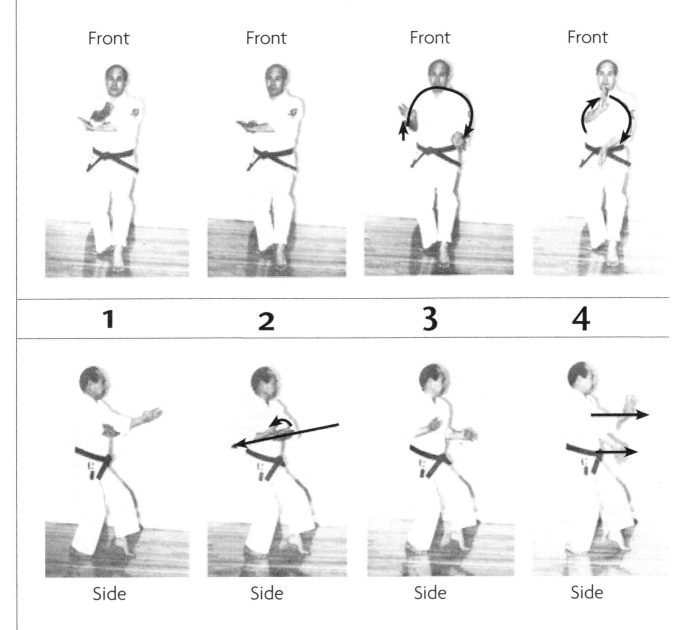

Front   Front   Front   Front

1   **2**   **3**   **4**

Side   Side   Side   Side

1. Standing in Neko-Ashi-Dachi stance with your left foot forward and your right arm semi-extended with the outer edge of your hand facing down and with your left open hand palm facing down below your right elbow.

2. Pull your right arm back.

3. Pivoting on your elbow move your left hand to the left side of your body in a circular motion and rotate your right wrist so that your fingers point up.

4. Continuing this circular motion move your right hand forward and to the middle of your body about shoulder height with your finger pointing up, and move your left hand forward and down to the middle of your body in front of your groin with your fingers pointing down. Your hands should form a vertical line.

KATA

Kata is a series of blocking, attacking and counter striking movements performed in succession in which all basic and advanced techniques of Karate are stored.

In olden times the techniques were secret and transferred from word of mouth. Because of a lack of reference a system which could store all the techniques was needed and so the Kata was invented to help the Karate student by engaging in imaginary combat against several opponents in different directions.

There are around 75 Katas, all different in complexity and duration. The Katas vary from very basic which cover all the Karate fundamentals to most advanced. It is of great importance that the basic katas are properly learned, for this will be the foundation on which the student will grow, in this way the student can avoid bad habits later on on more difficult Katas. With this in mind we can assume that the basic Katas are much more important than the advanced Katas, this is why it is important to have a good instructor.

The Katas for the advanced student require him to quickly change technique, speed, to not lose balance, extension and flexion of the body, a combination of hand, elbow, knee and leg techniques, conscious muscular tension and relaxation, breathing, and most important; concentration.

Katas are excellent tools for perfecting the student's abilities and for building strength and resistance.

Due to its enormous training value a student must better his Katas before concentrating on combat. to acquire precision and control the student must perform the Kata with good technique and in a rhythmical manner. The advanced Karate practitioner will acquire as much explosive strength and speed as it is possible and he will lose himself in the movement. Katas provide the opportunity to visualise your opponent and execute techniques without the restrictions that a partner or training match require, because of this Karate can only be effectively practiced through Kihon (basics) and Kata, of this Kata is the most effective.

The practice of Kata stimulates the analysis and control of each movement.

In conclusion we would like to present a quote about Kata from Master Kenwa Mabuni;

"The most important thing in karate are the Katas. In Katas all blocking and attacking techniques are intertwined. For this reason we must know its analytical meaning perfectly and practice them correctly."

Although some people believe that it is okay to ignore Kata and only practice combat (an analytical product of kata), this attitude will never get you very far in true Karate. That is because the striking and blocking techniques, the offensive and defensive techniques have thousands of variations which would be impossible to use in simple combat practice.

The abundance of appropriate training of the Katas its the best method for effective action in any situation. With this being said training only Kata is not enough, a variety of different training methods is needed to make the hand and feet techniques stronger and faster and to learn to change the stance or position as fast as possible to be more effective in a real situation.

One or two katas practiced correctly and to the point that they become part of yourself are everything a student needs. with other Kata functioning only for study or reference. A person may know all the Kata but they will be useless if they're not studied carefully studied. Learn and study profoundly just 2 or 3 Katas and when the moment comes, without you being conscious of it, this katas will be more effective than you ever imagined.

Another important point to think about is in the correct training method: if your training methods are incorrect it doesn't matter in how many fighting matches you've been or how many rocks or boards you try to break because your bad habits will bring defeat.

Even when Kata is the most important part of Karate you should not ignore the other aspects of karate such as fighting practice and the training of breaking rocks and boards. "The true effective way to Karate is to avoid idleness and futility and practice serously with the idea that Katas are 50 percent and the rest of your training is the other 50 percent."

Kata training is vital for the complete realization of the potential of Karate.

LIST OF SHITO RYU KATA

ITOSU-HA
JUNI NO KATA
HEIAN SHODAN
HEIAN NIDAN
HEIAN SANDAN
HEIAN JONDAN
HEIAN GODAN
JITTE
JIIN
JION
ROHAI SHODAN
ROHAI NIDAN
ROHAI SANDAN
BASSAI-DAI
BASSAI-SHO
KOSHOKUN-DAI
SHIHO KOSHOKUN
KOSHOKUN-SHO
CHINTEI
WANSHU
NAIFANCHIN SHODAN
NAIFANCHIN NIDAN
NAIFANCHIN SANDAN
CHINTO
GOJUSHIHO

HIGAONNA-HA
SANCHIN
TENSHO
SHISOCHIN
SEIENCHIN
SEIPAI
SAIFA
SEISAN
SANSERU
KURURUNFA
SUPARINPEI

MABUNI-HA
MIOJO
AOYAGI
JUROKU
MATSUKAZE

MATSUMURA-HA
ROHAI
BASSAI

TOMARI-TE
TOMARI NO PASSAI

ARAGAKI-HA
SOCHIN
UNSHU
NISEISHI

CHATANYARA
CHATANYARA KUSHANKU

OTHER
HAKUSHO
NIPAIPO
HAPOREN

MAKIWARA

While Kata is the heart of Karate, practice with the makiwara is the soul.

While the practice of Kata will teach you to move your body in the most efficient and effective way possible in combat, the constant practice with the makiwara will forge your fists and feet into lethal weapons making every technique much more effective and giving you the ability to end any confrontation with one single strike.

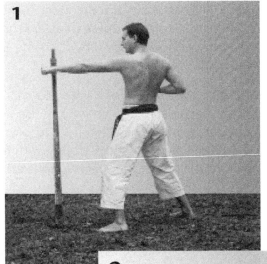

1. Stand in front of the Makiwara in Moto-Dachi stance with the front arm completely extended in front of you so that your wrist is touching the side of the Makiwara and the other arm is pulled back at the side of your body ready to strike.

2. Pull your front arm back while simultaneously throwing your fist to strike the Makiwara as in Gyaku-Zuki. Make sure to rotate your hip and push through the Makiwara after impact. Hold for one or two seconds and then return to the initial position and repeat.

Practice with the Makiwara should start slowly and gradually increase the force and repetitions applied to it until you are able to strike the makiwara with all your might. The number of repetitions has no limit, some masters are known to strike the Makiwara more than a thousand times with each arm, although three hundred reps is more than enough to build strong techniques.

With the practice of Makiwara the skin on the knuckles will tear and bleed, once this happens you should continue striking, overcoming physical pain and forging an unbreakable will. Soon the skin will become tougher and you will experience less pain making the practice easier. With enough practice, this tool will toughen your wrists and joints and make them stronger enabling you to deliver more power to your target, it will condition your body to react correctly in a confrontation and give you good timing, it will also teach you to contract and relax your body the correct way to deliver more power and generate more impact on contact (Kime).

"MISU ITAATE KYO NARU"

"SUITO KYO SEI"

"FROM A STRONG SPRING OF WATER
RIVERS ARE BORN"

"ZUI SHO NI SHU TO NARU"

"ALWAYS REMEMBER WHERE YOU WANT
TO GO AND STAY ON THAT PATH"

"PERSEVERANCE"

"ZUI SHO NI SHU TO NARU"

"FOLLOW YOUR OWN PATH,
MAKE YOUR OWN DECISIONS"

Made in the USA
Monee, IL
12 December 2022

20782242R00044